A Kid's Guide to

Greece

Jack L. Roberts
Michael Owens

Curious Kids Press • Palm Springs, CA
www.curiouskidspress.com

A WORD TO PARENTS

CURIOUS KIDS PRESS is passionate about helping young readers expand and enhance their understanding about countries and cultures around the world. While actual real-world experiences with other countries and cultures may have the most profound positive effect on children and pre-teens, we understand such experiences are not always possible. That's why our two series of books — "A Kid's Guide to . . ." (for ages 9-12) and "Let's Visit . . ." (for ages 6-8) — are designed to bridge that gap and help young readers explore the wonderful world of diversity in everything from food and holidays to geography and traditions. We hope your young explorers enjoy this adventure into the awesome country of Greece.

Cover Photo: The Kri-Kri Goat, found only on four islands of Greece. (*See page 39.*)
Page 1: The Meteora mountain and monastery, Greece.
Page 2: Santorini, Greece.

Publisher: Curious Kids Press, Palm Springs, CA 92264.
Designed by: Michael Owens
Editor: Sterling Moss
Copy Editor: Janice Ross

Table of Contents

Chapter 1

Welcome to Greece

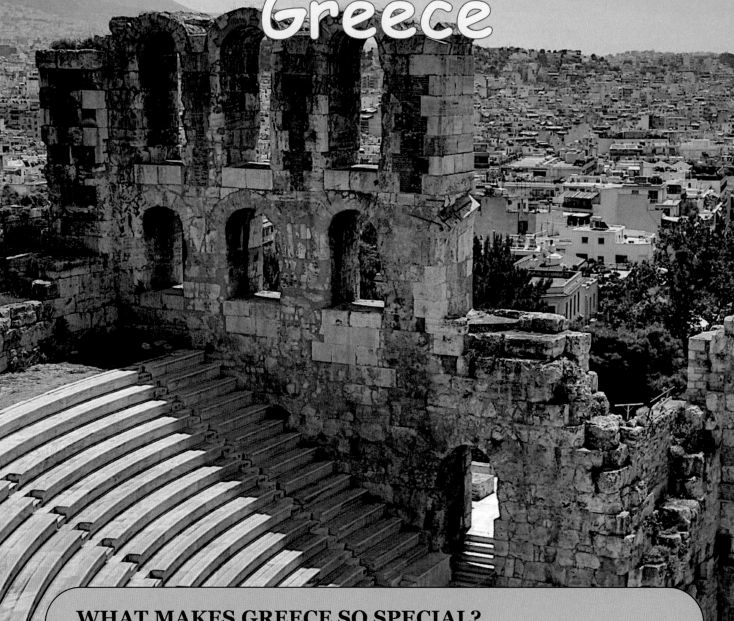

WHAT MAKES GREECE SO SPECIAL?

Sure, it's the home of the ancient Olympic Games. But did you know it's also considered the "cradle of Western civilization"? It's where many of the Western world's customs, beliefs, political systems, democracy and much more first got their start.

So, come along. Let's learn more about this amazing country.

Photo: *Old Olympic stadium in Athens, Greece.*

Your Passport to Greece

Official Name: Hellenic Republic (AKA Hellas).
Capital: Athens.
Country Area (Size): 50,942 sq. mi. (131,940 sq. km); a little smaller than the U.S. state of Louisiana.
Population: 10,761,523 (about the same as the U.S. state of Alabama).
Currency: Euro.
Official Language: Greek; English.

PASSPORT

THE NATIONAL FLAG OF GREECE (often called the "blue and white" for obvious reasons) has nine horizontal blue and white stripes, starting with blue at the top. On the upper left "hoist side" of the flag is a white cross. It **symbolizes** Eastern Orthodox Christianity. That's the main religion of the Greek people. According to tradition, the nine stripes represent the syllables in the Greek words for the motto "freedom or death."

Did You Know? Athens, the capital of Greece, was named for the goddess Athena.

Where in the World Is Greece?

GREECE IS A COUNTRY in Southeast Europe. It shares land borders with Albania to the northwest, North Macedonia and Bulgaria to the north, and Turkey to the northeast.

Greece is divided into four geographical regions: the mainland, the islands (about 6,000 of them), and two **peninsulas**: Peloponnese in the southwest and Chalkidiki in the northeast. The largest Greek island is Crete.

A Brief History of Ancient Greece

2,000 B.C. The first great civilization in Greece is established on the island of Crete. It's known as the Minoan civilization.

The Legend of Troy: 1194 B.C. and 1184 B.C:

Perhaps, the best-known **legend** in Greece is the Legend of Ancient Troy. In the legend, a ten-year war was waged between the Greeks and the Trojans (the people of Troy). It lasted between 1194 B.C. and 1184 B.C.

The legend tells how the Greeks conquered the city of Troy by hiding inside a giant wooden horse. The people of Troy thought the horse was a gift and brought it inside the city's walls. But inside the horse were the Greek soldiers who slipped out of the horse and seized (or took control of) the city.

800 B.C : The Greeks start to split their land into city-states, each with its own laws and ruler. The largest city-states were Athens, Sparta, and Thebes.

146 B.C: The Romans conquer the Greeks.

508 B.C.

Athens begins a new system of government by the people called democracy. But only men could vote.

776 B.C.: The first Olympic Games are held in the southern city of Olympia. Only men are allowed to compete.

393 A.D. Roman Emperor Theodosius bans future Olympics.

146 B.C: The Romans conquer the Greeks.

Classical Greece

When most people think of Ancient Greece, they think about a two-hundred-year period between 508 B.C. and 323 B.C.

Today, this period is known as Classical Greece. It's a time when Athens was governed by a democracy.

It's a time when great philosophers like Socrates and Plato wrote. It was also the time of the wars between Sparta and Athens. This period ended with the rise and then death of Alexander the Great in 323 BC.

1821-1830: Greek revolutionaries wage the Greek War of Independence against the Ottoman Empire.

1832: Greece wins its independence.

1896: The first modern Olympic Games are held in Athens. A total of 213 athletes from 13 nations compete in 43 events.

1975: Greece **abolishes** its monarchy and becomes a **parliamentary republic.**

2004: Athens hosts the 2004 Summer Olympics. It was the first time Greece hosted the Olympics since 1896, the year of the first Modern Olympics.

Cool Facts About Greece

Mount Olympus is the highest mountain in Greece. It is 9,570 feet (2,917 meters) above sea level. BTW, the highest mountain on Earth is Mount Everest at 29,029 feet (8,848 m).

Have you ever heard the funny saying: "It's raining cats and dogs"? It means it is raining really hard.

So, what do they say in Greece when it's raining hard?

Vrékhi kareklopódara!

It means "it's raining chair legs."

Now, that's really a funny saying.

The 5 Biggest Cities (by population) in Greece

City	Population
Athens	664,046
Thessaloniki	315,196
Patras	167,446
Piraeus	163,688
Larissa	144,651

Coastline

Greece has the longest coastline in Europe.

TUESDAY THE 13ᵀᴴ

In the U. S. and other parts of the world, many people are superstitious about Friday the 13th. They think it is an unlucky day.

But in Greece the "unlucky" day is Tuesday the 13th.

National Anthem

The Greek National Anthem (*Hymn to Liberty*) is the longest in the world. It was written in 1823 and consisted of 58 verses. But in 1865, because it was so long, the Greek Government adopted the first two stanzas as the official anthem.

Greek Superlatives

Greece is full of superlatives—you know, oldest, longest, tallest—those kinds of things. Here are some of them.

• Athens, the capital of Greece, is the **OLDEST** capital city in Europe.

• Mount Olympus is the **HIGHEST** mountain in Greece (9,570 ft/2,917 m).

• The River Haliacmon is the **LONGEST** river in Greece (185 miles/297 km).

• Greece has the **LONGEST** coastline in the Mediterranean (8,498 miles/13,676 km).

Olive Growers

Greece is among the top three olive producing countries in the world. It produces more than two million tons of olives a year. Spain, however, is the number one producer of olives. It produces more than five million tons.

Did You Know?

The first Greek to win a Gold Medal at the Modern Olympics was King Constantine II, though he wasn't king at the time. He won a gold medal in sailing at the 1960 Olympics. In 1964, he became king. He's still king (as of 2020) but he doesn't have any power in governing the country. That's because in 1974 the monarchy was abolished.

GREEK INDEPENDENCE DAY
March 25
It **commemorates** the start of the War of Greek Independence in 1821. The motto of the revolutions was "Freedom or Death."
In celebration of Greek Independence Day each year, school kids march in a parade in traditional Greek costume and carry Greek flags.

National Sport

Football (soccer in the United States) is the national sport of Greece.

People, Customs And Traditions

GREEK CULTURE has developed over thousands of years. Today, Greece's rich history influences many of the customs and traditions of Greek life, including music, holidays, religion, food, politics, and much more.

Folk Dancers from several countries taking part in the Annual Folk Dance festival in the village square of Pefkohori, Greece.

Greek people are extremely patriotic. They take a great deal of pride in their country. They also put a great deal of importance on family life.

But if there is one Greek word that best describes the Greek people, it's *philotimo*. It's not a word that is easily translated in English. But, in general, it means "love of honor." It has to do with always doing the right thing or thinking of others first before yourself.

Carnival

IN MANY COUNTRIES AROUND THE WORLD, the forty-day period before Easter is known Lent. It is a time for a colorful and lively celebration, known as Carnival.

In Greece, Carnival is called "Apokries." It's a time when the streets of many cities and towns are filled with elaborate costumes, grand parades, and other colorful festivities.

The most famous Carnival in Greece is the Big Carnival of Patras, Greece's third largest city. Hundreds of thousands of visitors come to Patras for the celebration.

People dress in costume, play games and jokes, have a huge parade, and throw sweets to the people. There are treasure hunts for kids and even a special children's carnival.

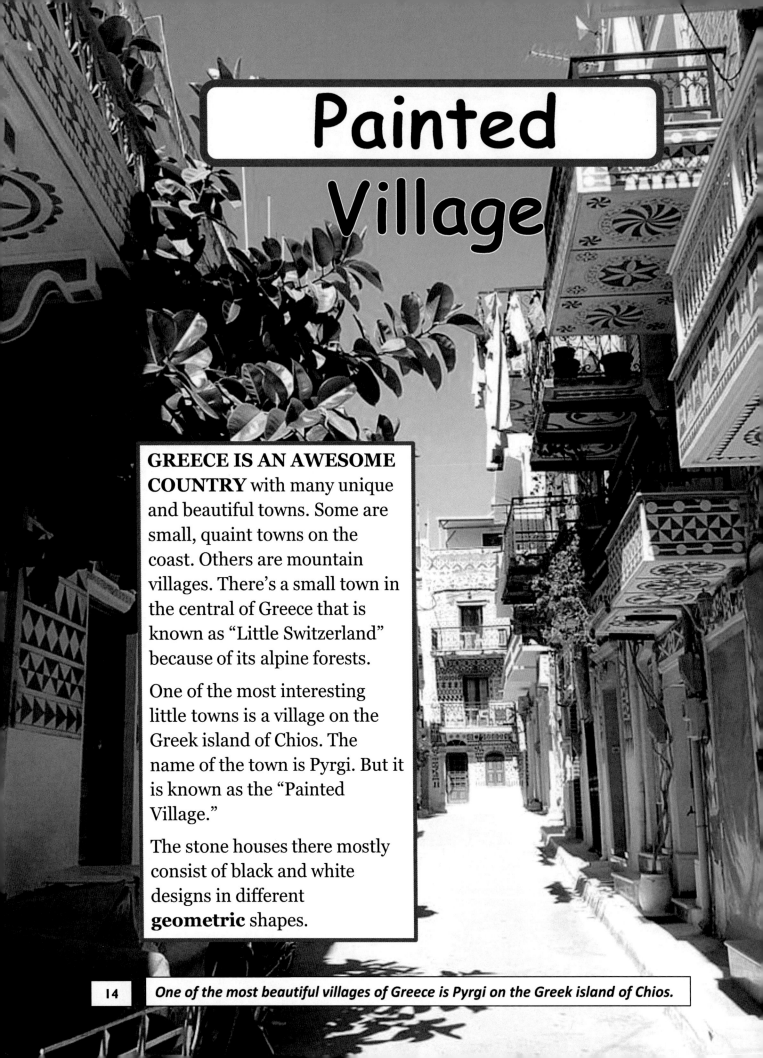

Painted Village

GREECE IS AN AWESOME COUNTRY with many unique and beautiful towns. Some are small, quaint towns on the coast. Others are mountain villages. There's a small town in the central of Greece that is known as "Little Switzerland" because of its alpine forests.

One of the most interesting little towns is a village on the Greek island of Chios. The name of the town is Pyrgi. But it is known as the "Painted Village."

The stone houses there mostly consist of black and white designs in different **geometric** shapes.

One of the most beautiful villages of Greece is Pyrgi on the Greek island of Chios.

The Greek Alphabet And Symbols

GREEK IS ONE OF THE OLDEST languages in the world. There are 24 letters in the Greek alphabet. The English word *alphabet* actually comes from the first two letters in the Greek alphabet: *alpha* and *beta*.

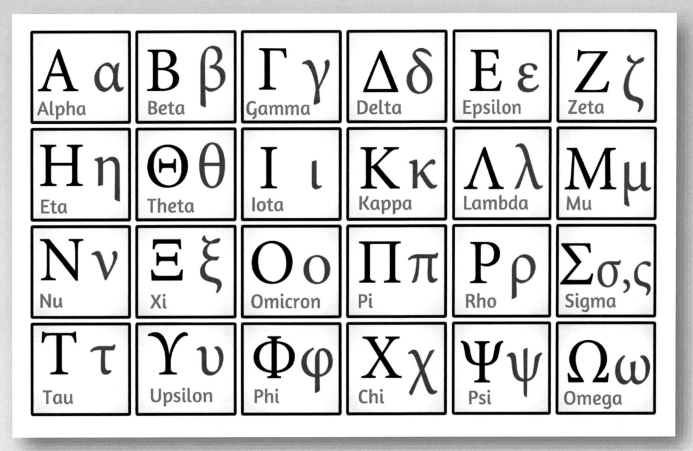

Today, many English words come from Greek words. For example, did you know the word *hippopotamus* comes from two Greek words? *Hippo* in Greek means horse; *potamos* means river. So, hippopotamus means river horse or horse of the river. And guess what. A hippopotamus lives mostly in and close to water.

Greek Folkdances

THE GREEKS LOVE TO DANCE. And they have a lot of different dances to choose from. In fact, there are more than 4,000 traditional Greek dances that are popular in all different regions of the country. Many of the dances got their start in Ancient Greece in the days of Plato and Aristotle.

But one of the most popular Greek dances, however, isn't nearly that old. It's called *Sirtaki*, and it got its start in 1964. It was created for a movie called *Zorba the Greek*. That's why the dance is sometimes called Zorba's Dance or just Zorba's.

Sirtaki is danced in a line with each dancer's hands placed on the shoulders of the dancers next to them. It starts slow and builds to a fast pace. It often includes hops and leaps.

A Guessing Game

HOW MANY PEOPLE do you think have ever danced the Sirtaki together at one time?

If you said 5,614, you're right. On August 31, 2012, 5,614 people, ages 14 to 89, danced the Sirtaki for five minutes by the sea in the city of Volvos, Greece.

They broke a "Sirtaki Dance" Guinness World Record.

Greek Food

How many of these favorite Greek foods have you tried?

Dolma (stuffed grape leaves)

Classic Greek salad

Greek Christmas appetizer

Meat pies

Pita bread with spinach

GREEK CUISINE

Salad with octopus

Garlic bread

Stuffed eggplant rolls

Stuffed squid with rice

Evzones

HAVE YOU EVER TRIED to stand perfectly still for five minutes? It's not easy, is it?

Now imagine standing without moving (and without showing any expressions on your face) for an hour at a time.

That's what a special group of Greek soldiers do every day. They are known as the "Evzones." They are the Greek Presidential Guard.

The Evzones stand guard every day at the Tomb of the Unknown Soldier and the Presidential Mansion in Greece. The "changing of the guards" takes place every hour on the hour, 24 hours a day They stand completely still until it is time to switch with another guard.

To be an Evzone requires special training. Evzones have to learn how to stand perfectly still. They also have to learn to march in unison. Their movements must match. They must be able to raise their legs to shoulder height, completely straight, as they march back and forth each day.

A lot of soldiers apply to be an Evzone. But almost half of all *chosen* candidates fail to complete the training.

Those that do succeed are paired up with a "brother," usually someone who looks very much like them. They stand guard together, and if one is unable to attend to his duties, the other does not stand guard with anyone else.

Evzones are not allowed to speak to anyone when they are on duty. A regular soldier stands nearby. If someone tries to attack or touch an Evzone, the soldier steps in and stops it.

Did You Know?

Evzones wear a special white pleated skirt called a *foustanella*. Each skirt has 400 pleats. The number of pleats symbolizes the number of years that Greece was under the control of the Ottoman Empire.

The Story of Ancient Greece

The Ancient Greece city-states were often at war. But every four years, just before the Olympics, they would call a truce, so everyone could travel to the Olympics safely.

ANCIENT GREECE WAS NOT a united country with one king or leader. Instead, it was made up of lots of city-states. Each city-state had its own ruler and its own form of government.

The two most powerful city-states were Athens and Sparta.

Athens was the largest and most powerful city-state. It produced many writers, artists, architects, and philosophers. Their work is well-known today.

Athens was also the birthplace of democracy. The people believed that they should be able to choose government officials and vote for or against new laws.

Athens was named after the Greek goddess Athena.

Sparta is well-known for its military strength. It had a very strong army. Beginning at age seven, Spartan boys trained to become warriors.

Spartan society was divided into three classes of people.

• **The Spartan Citizen**. There were relatively few Spartan citizens. Spartan citizens were those people whose direct ancestors formed the city of Sparta. •

The Perioikoi. These were free people who lived in Spartan lands. They could travel, own land, and conduct business. But they were not Spartan citizens.

• The **Helots.** This was the largest group of people in Sparta. They were slaves or serfs to the Spartans.

The Greek Gods

THE ANCIENT GREEKS had many gods and goddesses. The Greeks built temples and offered **sacrifices** to their major gods. The people also told many different stories about these gods and goddesses.

Many ancient Greeks believed these stories were true. But others thought the stories were fiction or not true. Today, these stories and legends are known as myths or Greek mythology.

Many of the stories in Greek mythology were about the twelve major gods. These gods lived on Mount Olympus. Here is brief description of each of those twelve gods and goddesses.

 **ZEUS** was the king of the gods. He was also the strongest and wisest and ruled over the earth. He controlled the weather. His two brothers were Poseidon and Hades.

 **POSEIDON** was the god of the seas. He was also the god of earthquakes and horses. He carried a three-point spear called a trident. He could be very **temperamental**.

 **HERMES** was the young and intelligent messenger god. Whenever the gods wanted to send messages to mortals, they gave the job to Hermes. He carried a magic wand. His father was Zeus.

The Greek god **HADES** ruled the Underworld, the world of the dead. Neither gods nor mortals liked Hades very much. He lived in the Underworld, rather than on Mount Olympus.

ATHENA was the goddess of wisdom. She was also a great warrior. She was always seen with a shield and spear. Her father was Zeus.

APOLLO and his sister Artemis were twins. Apollo was the god of wisdom, poetry, and music. He also loved hunting.

APHRODITE was the goddess of love. She married Hephaestus, but was really in love with Ares. She liked making people fall in love.

ARTEMIS was the goddess of the moon and the hunt. She liked to protect wildlife.

HEPHAESTUS was the god of fire. He was a blacksmith whose **forge** was in a volcano. He was good-natured and got along with everyone.

ARES was the god of war, even though Athena was a much better warrior. In fact, he was considered more of a bully than a warrior. He liked to watch people fight.

DEMETER was the goddess of agriculture. She could make plants grow (or not grow). People worshipped her because they depended on her for good crops.

HERA was the beautiful queen of the gods and protector of women. She was very vain about her looks

The Ancient Greeks agreed that twelve Greek gods had thrones on Mt. Olympus. They agreed on who eleven of these gods were. But they couldn't agree on who the twelfth one was. It was either Hestia, the oldest of the gods, or Dionysus, the god of wine and celebrations.

HESTIA

DIONYSUS

Pericles and The Golden Age of Athens

IMAGINE A CITY with all the excitement of London, Paris, and New York rolled into one.

To a great extent, that's what Athens was like between 478 B.C. and 404 B.C.—a time we now call "the Golden Age of Athens."

During this period, Athens produced some of the greatest playwrights, historians, and philosophers, such as Plato or Aristotle.

Pericles was often called the First citizen of Athens.

But perhaps one of the greatest achievements during this time was in architecture. And the person most responsible for the construction of many of the great buildings was a statesman and **orator** by the name of Pericles (PAIR-uh-kleez).

Pericles was responsible for rebuilding many temples on the acropolis. He was also responsible for the construction of the Parthenon. He also had the Long Walls built from Athens to its two main seaports.

Pericles believed every person had the right to take part in government, not just wealthy citizens. He also encouraged education and the arts. He worked to help establish Athens as the leader of the Greek World.

The leadership of Pericles ushered in a time that is called the Golden Age of Athens. Today, it is also known as the Age of Pericles.

Pericles

The Greek Hall of

ANCIENT GREECE was one of the greatest **civilizations** in history, thanks in large part to its many great historians, philosophers, playwrights, scientists, and statesmen. Here are just some of them.

GREEK PHILOSOPHERS

SOCRATES
(About 470 BC-399 BC)
Philosopher
Founder of Western philosophy.

PLATO
(About 428/427 BC-348/347 BC)
Philosopher/scholar
Founded the Academy in Athens.

ARISTOTLE
(384-322 BC)
Philosopher/scholar
Founded the Lyceum.

GREEK STATESMAN/LEADERS

ALEXANDER THE GREAT
(356-323 BC)
Military Leader
Often called the greatest military leader in the world.

DEMOSTHENES
(384-322 BC)
Statesman/Orator
Greatest orator (public speaker) of his time.

PERICLES
(About 495 BC-429 BC)
Statesman
Promoted democracy; led the building of many great structures.

The Ancient Greeks loved plays. Almost every city had a theater. But only men and boys could be actors, no women or girls were allowed on the stage.

GREEK PLAYWRIGHTS/POETS

ARISTOPHANES
(448-380 BC)
Playwright
Father of the comedy

AESCHYLUS
(525-456 BC)
Playwright
Father of the tragedy

HOMER
(Unknown)
Poet
Composed the epic poems the *Iliad* and the *Odyssey*.

GREEK HISTORIAN

HERODOTUS
(About 485 BC-425 BC)
Historian
Often called the Father of History

GREEK MATHEMATICIANS/ SCIENTISTS

ARCHIMEDES
(About 287 BC-212 BC)
Mathematician
Considered one of the greatest mathematicians in history.

EUCLID
(Unknown)
Scholar
Father of Geometry.

PYTHAGORAS
(580-500 BC)
Scientist and philosopher
Famous for theory in geometry

GREEK DOCTORS

HIPPOCRATES
(460-377 BC)
Physician
Called the Father of Western Medicine

The idea that planets orbit the sun was first thought of by an ancient Greek astronomer and mathematician named Aristarchus of Samos.

An Imaginary Aristotle

ANCIENT GREECE produced some of the world's best thinkers, writers, and philosophers. One of the best was Aristotle. Here is an imaginary conversation with this great philosopher. If you could ask Aristotle a question, what would you ask?

When and where were you born?

I was born in 384 B.C. in Stagira, a small town on the northern coast of Greece. My father was the doctor to the king of Greece.

Did you go to school as a kid?

I was what you would call today home-schooled. I had tutors who taught me all sorts of subjects.

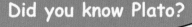

Did you know Plato?

For sure. When I was 17 years old, I enrolled in Plato's Academy in Athens. I stayed there for 20 years, first as a student and later as a teacher.

26

What was The Lyceum?

It was a school I started when I was about 50 years old. In a way, it was like today's universities. But we didn't have classrooms. Instead, my students would follow me around. We would talk about and debate important issues.

What did you do after you left Plato's Academy?

I was about 37 years old at the time. I traveled throughout Greece and Turkey, got married, and wrote several books about animals. I was probably the first to classify different types of animals into different groups.

Plato gave you the nickname "The Mind" because you were so smart. But did you ever get anything wrong?

Oh, sure. Lots of things. For example, I thought the heart was the center of intelligence, not the brain. Oops!

27

Chapter 3

Landmarks and The Acropolis

IN GREEK, THE WORD ACROPOLIS means "high city." Throughout Greece, there are many acropolises (or acropoleis). But the best known is the Acropolis of Athens. Most people think of it as simply The Acropolis.

The Acropolis of Athens is a flat-topped rock that measures about 7 1/2 acres. That's about the size of seven football fields put together. It is 512 feet (150 m) above sea level.

Pericles, an important Greek statesman and orator, was responsible for building most of the important structures on the Acropolis. His work covered a period between 461 B.C. and 429 B.C., a time often called "the Age of Pericles."

The remains of eleven of those structures still stand today. The Parthenon is the most famous. (*See page xx.*)

The Acropolis of Athens.

Propylaea

IN GREEK, the word **propylaea** is the name given to huge gates or entranceways to a specific space, usually to a temple or religious complex.

The most famous and best-preserved example of this type of structure is the magnificent Propylaea of the Acropolis of Athens.

The Parthenon

The Parthenon crowns the Acropolis in Athens.

THE PARTHENON IS THE NAME of a marble temple that was built to honor the Greek goddess Athena, the goddess of wisdom and courage. It was built in the 5th century B.C. between 447 B.C. and 432 B.C.

The structure sits on the hill of the Acropolis at Athens. It is a magnificent example of ancient Greek architecture. It measures approximately 101 feet (31 meters) wide by 228 feet (70 meters) long. By comparison, the White House in Washington, D.C., measures 152 feet wide (46.3 meters) by 168 feet (51.2 meters) long.

The Parthenon has 46 Doric columns that supported the roof, 8 across the front and back and 17 on each side. They are 34 feet (10.4 meters) high. The structure also had 23 inner columns.

The Parthenon was elaborately decorated with marble sculptures both inside and out. Unfortunately, only a few of these sculptures still exist today. For example, the area above the columns on the "front" of the Parthenon depicts the birth of Athena. On the "back" of the temple, a sculpture shows Athena's battle with Poseidon for ownership of the land of Attica (an area that includes Athens).

Today, the Parthenon is considered a **symbol** of the Ancient Greek world. It is also one of the most famous structures in the world.

The Temple of Apollo

THE TEMPLE OF APOLLO at Delphi was the center of a large sacred site on the slopes of Mt. Parnassus, a mountain in central Greece.

The ruins of the temple consist of six Doric columns and a multi-layered platform of stones.

A view of the theater at Delphi and the remains of the Temple of Apollo

Today, a marble walkway winds its way up to the ruins of this great temple from the Agora, the Ancient Greek marketplace. The path is known as the Sacred Way. In Ancient Greece, it was lined with special marble and bronze statues, where people could leave special offerings.

Fifteen hundred feet above the temple is an impressive amphitheater. It's known as the **Ancient Theater of Delphi**. Musical events were held there as part of the Pythian Games, which were held to honor Apollo.

The Pythian Games were held at the **Ancient Stadium of Delphi** above the theater. The stadium is considered the best-preserved monument of its kind in the world.

Why Apollo's Sanctuary at Delphi Was Important

Delphi was an international, neutral meeting place among the separate Greek city states. At Delphi, the leaders of the different city states could negotiate deals, settle disputes, conduct rituals, and even consult the Oracle. It was a place of diplomacy.

The Temple of Apollo from the 4th Century B.C.

Photo: Helen Simonsson

Erechtheum Temple

A view from the south of the Erechtheum temple on the Acropolis in Athens.

THE ERECHTHEUM TEMPLE on the Acropolis in Athens is the second largest temple on the Acropolis. It was built between 421 B.C. and 406 B.C., and was **dedicated** to both Athena and Poseidon, the god of the sea. It was named after the legendary Greek hero, Erichthonius.

The structure features **ionic capitals,** which many people say are the most beautiful that Ancient Greece produced.

The temple is famous, in part, for its Porch of the Maidens (or Porch of the Caraytis). The porch features the statues of six Greek female figures (caryatids) that help to support the structure.

The Greek Columns

The Ancient Greeks were great architects. They invented, among other things, three types of columns to support their structures. They include:

• **Doric:** This column was wider at the bottom than at the top. It was simple in design. The capital (or top) of the column was square-ish and plain.

• **Ionic:** This column was thinner than the Doric. The capital at the top was decorated with scrolls on each side.

• **Corinthian**: This column was the most decorative. The capital featured elaborate scrolls and ornaments (or decorations) that were carved to look like acanthus leaves (see photo).

These three styles are still used in many buildings today.

Acanthus leaves.

Example of Corinthian capital. Does it look like acanthus leaves?

The Windmills of Mykonos

THE ISLAND OF MYKONOS—known as "The Island of the Wind"— is about 95 miles (153 km) from the mainland. It has land area of 33 sq. miles (85.5 sq. km), which is about half the size of the land area of the District of Columbia in the United States.

Mykonos is known for its many beautiful sandy beaches. But it is also known for its windmills. There are currently 16 windmills on Mykonos. Most of them were built in the 16th century. Back then, they were used to grind wheat and barley to make flour. The oldest windmill was still producing flour in the 1960s. Today, some of the windmills have been turned into houses.

Chapter 4

The Animals of Greece

GREECE HAS AN INCREDIBLE VARIETY of wildlife, including dozens of different kinds of birds, numerous amphibians and reptiles, and nearly one hundred **species** of **mammals.**

Approximately twenty of the mammals of Greece are considered endangered (at risk of **extinction**). One is the Kri-Kri goat. (*See page 39*). Many organizations in Greece work to protect these endangered species.

Greece is also home to a large number of species of birds. Some live all year round in Greece. Some come to Greece to breed and raise their young. And some just spend the winter in Greece to escape colder conditions elsewhere.

For each of the animals of Greece pictured in this chapter, be sure to check out its "conservation status" in the red box . See the explanation of "conservation status" on the next page.

The European Bee-eater

European Bee-eater
Conservation Status: LC

Photo: Charles J. Sharp

One of the most colorful (and many say the most beautiful) birds to visit Greece each year is the European Bee-eater. These birds usually fly from Africa to Greece in the spring to breed. They build their nests in holes in the ground near rivers or lakes. Each of the three European bee-eaters in this photo holds a dragonfly in its mouth.

The European Mink

About one hundred years ago, the European mink was found throughout Europe. Today, the population is declining rapidly. The decline is due mainly to hunting, habitat loss, and water pollution. Small populations still exist in Spain and France.

European Mink Conservation Status: EN in Greece

Photo: Nicolai Meyer

The face of the European mink has white markings on the upper lip, unlike the American species.

The IUCN Red List

IUCN stands for the International Union for the Conservation of Nature. The IUCN Red List tells how likely it is that a certain **species** (plant or animal) might become **extinct in the future.** This is called its conservation status and consists of six categories:

Least Concern (LC): Unlikely to become extinct in the near future.

Near Threatened (NT): Close to high risk of extinction in the near future.

Vulnerable (VU): Considered to be at high risk of extinction.

Endangered (EN): Considered to be at very high risk in the wild.

Critically Endangered (CR): In an extremely critical state of future extinction.

Extinct in the Wild (EW): Exists in captivity.

The Kri-kri Goat

The Kri-Kri Goat
Conservation Status: EN

THIS MAMMAL is found only on the Greek island of Crete (and three nearby smaller islands). Maybe that's why it's also known as the Cretan goat. It's the largest mammal on the island.

Males typically have a beard. They have a black line on their back. It runs from the neck to the top of the tail. Scientists believe the Kri-kri goat was brought to the island from Persia thousands of years ago.

KRI-KRI GOAT
At-a-Glance

Size: Small to medium.

Weight: Buck: Up to 198 lbs. (90 kg); Doe: Up to 92 lbs. (42 kg).

Horns: Yes. They sweep back from their heads.

Population: About 2,000 on Crete.

Other: They can leap huge distances and climb sheer cliffs.

The Dalmatian Pelican

THE DALMATIAN PELICAN
At-a-Glance

Stands: Up to 4 ft. (1.20 m) tall.

Length: Up to 6 ft. (1.8 m).

Wingspan: Up to 10 ft. 6 in (3.2 m)

Weight: Up to 33 lbs. (15 kg).

Population: Fewer than 20,000.

Other: Both parents take turns feeding their chicks (baby pelicans).

Dalmatian Pelican
Conservation Status: NT

WHEN YOU HEAR THE WORD "DALMATIAN," you probably think of a large dog with a white coat and black spots.

But did you know there is a "dalmatian" in Greece that is not a dog... it's a bird...a pelican to be exact?

The dalmatian pelican is rarest of seven different kinds (or species) of pelicans in the world. It is also the second biggest bird species on the planet.

Photo:Thomas Bresson, Belfort, France

The Mediterranean Monk Seal

THE MONK SEAL is a very rare breed. In fact, scientists estimate there are only about 600 monk seals left in the wild. That's why when scientists discover a new colony of monk seals, they keep it a secret to protect the animals.

Monk seals typically live in sea caves. They are generally shy and try to avoid human contact.

THE MEDITERRANEAN MONK SEAL
At-a-Glance

Length: Up to 7.9 feet (2.4 m) long.

Weight: Up to 710 lb. (320 kg).

Average Lifespan: 20-25 years/

Diet: Fish: octopus, squid, and eel.

The Mediterranean Monk Seal
Conservation Status: EN

The Dolphin
The National Animal of Greece

Did You Know? Dolphins are not fish. So, what are they? They're mammals. Yet, they can "store" enough oxygen in their lungs to swim underwater for twenty minutes.

DOLPHINS ARE FASCINATING CREATURES. Scientists say their brain is as complicated as a human brain. They have great eyesight and hearing. Some say they also have a great sense of humor.

In Ancient Greece, dolphins were highly respected. In fact, it was considered a crime to kill a dolphin, punishable by death.

Today, Dolphins are considered the national animal of Greece.

THERE ARE 32 DFFERENT species (or kinds) of dolphins in the world. Four of them live in the waters around Greece.

- **The common bottlenose dolphin**, a playful dolphin. It is the one that you are likely to see near the shore. Conservation Status: LC

- **The common dolphin**. Surprise. It's not very common at all. It can swim very fast, reaching 65 km per hour. Conservation Status: EN

- **The striped dolphin**, the most common type of dolphin. It has a black stripe starting from its eye to its tail. Striped dolphins are rarely seen because they like the very deep sea. Conservation Status: VU

- **The Risso's dolphin**, the largest of the four. It can reach nearly 10 feet (3 meters) in length. Conservation Status: LC

Striped dolphins in the Gulf of Corinth

The Legend of the Dolphin

The Ancient Greeks had many stories or legends. One is about the dolphin and Dionysus, the god of wine and pleasure.

According to this legend, Dionysus took on the appearance of a young **mortal** to sail to the island of Naxos. On the way, he overheard the crew plotting to sell him as a slave. So, he turned the oars into **serpents**. The sailors had no choice but to jump overboard.

Poseidon, the god of the sea, took pity on them. He turned the sailors into dolphins. He then gave them the task of helping seamen in danger everywhere.

The Loggerhead Turtle

THE LOGGERHEAD TURTLE is common in Greece, mainly around the island of Crete. Hundreds of loggerheads lay their eggs on Crete's sandy beaches every summer.

Loggerheads are the largest hard-shelled turtles in the world. They are protected by law in Greece.

Sadly, many loggerheads die as a result of swallowing plastic bags that they think are jellyfish.

The Loggerhead Sea Turtle
Conservation Status: EN

Photo: Brian Gratwicke

THE LOGGERHEAD TURTLE
At-a-Glance

Length: Up to 48 inches (122 cm).

Weight: Up to 330 lbs. (150 kg).

Lifespan: 47- 67 years.

Diet: Mainly jellyfish.

Other: They are called loggerheads because of their large heads.

Glossary

abolish (*verb*): To end; put a stop to; do away with.

civilization (*noun*): The culture and achievements of a society; the advanced state of development of a society.

commemorate (*verb*): To serve as a reminder of or to honor the memory of.

culture (*noun*): The language, customs, beliefs, and art of a particular group of people.

dedicated (*adjective*): Supporting something, such as a cause or goal; believing in something.

democracy (*noun*): A form of government in which the power is with the people.

independence (*noun*): Freedom from outside control; self-sufficient.

Ionic, Doric, Corinthian: Three styles of Greek columns, each with grooves down the side called fluting, and each with a distinctive capital (the top part of the column).

> **Doric**: simple, square capital.

> **Ionic**: capital with scrolls on each side.

> **Corinthian**: capital designed to look like leaves of the acanthus plant.

forge (*noun*): A place like a furnace or hearth where metal is heated.

legend (*noun*): A popular story handed down from generation to generation that cannot be proven.

monarchy (*noun*): Government by a ruler (king or queen) who may hold all power or whose power is limited by a constitution.

mortal (*noun*): A human being.

myth (*noun*): A story based on a tradition or legend.

orator (*noun*): A person who has skill in public speaking.

parliamentary republic: A form of government in which the people elect their representatives (the parliament) and the parliament chooses the executive.

peninsula (*noun*): An area of land surrounded by water on all sides except for a narrow strip of land connected to the mainland.

sacrifice (*noun*): The offering of some living thing or material possession to a deity as an act of worship.

serpent (noun): Snake.

symbolize (*verb*): To represent by means of a symbol, such as a sign or figure or emblem.

underworld (*noun*): An imaginary region inhabited by the dead.

Explore the World

Find these books on Amazon.com
Preview them at curiouskidspress.com

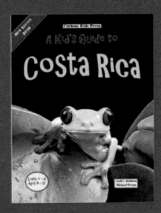

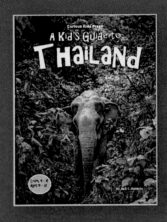
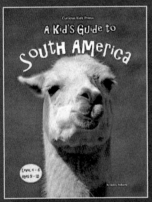

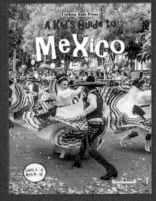
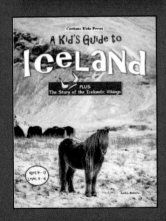

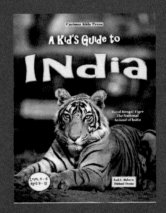

Curious Kids Press
www.curiouskidspress.com

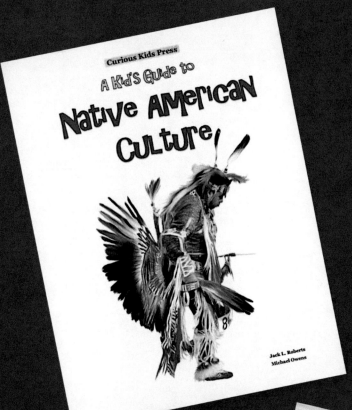

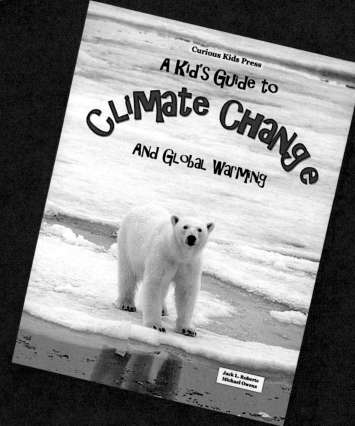

Two important new books for all young readers and their families.

Available on amazon.com

A Kid's Guide to
Greece
For Parents and Teachers

About This Book

A Kid's Guide to . . . is an engaging, easy-to-read book series that provides an exciting adventure into fascinating countries and cultures around the world for young readers. Each book focuses on one country, continent, or U.S. territory or state, and includes colorful photographs, informational charts and graphs, and quirky and bizarre "Did You Know" facts, all designed to bring the country and its people to life. Designed primarily for recreational, high-interest reading, the informational text series is also a great resource for students to use to research geography topics or writing assignments.

About the Reading Level

A Kid's Guide to . . . is an informational text series designed for kids in grades 4 to 6, ages 9 to 12. For some young readers, the series will provide new reading challenges based on the vocabulary and sentence structure. For other readers, the series will review and reinforce reading skills already achieved. While for still other readers, the book will match their current skill level, regardless of age or grade level.

About the Authors

Jack L. Roberts began his career in educational publishing at Children's Television Workshop (now Sesame Workshop), where he was Senior Editor of The Sesame Street/Electric Company Reading Kits. Later, at Scholastic Inc., he was the founding editor of a high-interest/low-reading level magazine for middle school students. He also founded two technology magazines for teachers and administrators.

Roberts is the author of more than two dozen biographies and other nonfiction titles for young readers, published by Scholastic Inc., the Lerner Publishing Group, Teacher Created Materials, Benchmark Education, and others.. More recently, he was the co-founder of WordTeasers, an educational series of card decks designed to help kids of all ages improve their vocabulary through "conversation, not memorization."

Michael Owens is a noted jazz dance teacher, award-winning wildlife photographer, graphic arts designer, and devoted animal lover.

In 2017, Roberts and Owens launched Curious Kids Press (CKP), an educational publishing company focused on publishing high-interest, nonfiction books for young readers, primarily books about countries and cultures around the world. Currently, CKP has published two series of country books: "A Kid's Guide to..." (for ages 9-12 and "Let's Visit . . ." (for ages 6-8) — both designed to help young readers explore the wonderful world of diversity in everything from food and holidays to geography and traditions.

To Our Valued Customers

Curious Kids Press is passionate about creating fun-to-read books about countries and cultures around the world for young readers, and we work hard every day to create quality products.

All of our books are Print on Demand books. As a result, on rare occasions, you may find minor printing errors. If you feel you have not received a quality printed product, please send us a description and photo of the printing error along with your name and address and we will have a new copy sent to you free of charge. Contact us at: info@curiouskidspress.com

Made in the USA
Middletown, DE
04 May 2022